V . O . I . C . E . In The Classroom

10 Steps Toward Self-Reliant Writing

© Suzanne Rothman
Written and designed by Suzanne Rothman

V . O . I . C . E .

Decide The Number of Days Per Lesson Based on Your Unique Learners
Every Step has room for Complexity

Step 1   Lesson Set Up and Anchor Chart

Step 2   **V**oice

Step 3   **O**rganization

Step 4   **I**deas

Step 5   **C**onventions

Step 6   **E**xpression

Step 7   Modeling Brainstorm & Flow of Thought

Step 8   Errors and Revisions In Motion

Step 9   Rough Draft In Layers

Step 10   Connect The Dots

Notes, questions, and ideas to make your V.O.I.C.E. stronger:

Lesson Set-Up and Anchor Chart

Begin with teacher- written notes, not a hand-out. Write an outline or synoposis of V.O.I.C.E. notes on a large classroom board. These notes work well when accompanied by teacher read aloud of notes. Students need to copy clear and accurate notes.

After students copy and hear notes, the teacher should create an Anchor Chart of V.O.I.C.E. with students. Students in whole group assist teacher with the first Anchor Chart by referring to their notes, giving verbal contributions of the elements of V.O.I.C.E. and watching as the teacher puts together the Anchor Chart.

Reinforce the lesson by having students create a V.O.I.C.E. Anchor Chart in groups without their notes or teacher Anchor Chart. Group Anchor Charts are successful at each stage of V.O.I.C.E when discussed as a class. Ask students to compare. Does every student Anchor Chart clearly contain all the elements of V.O.I.C.E.? Fix accordingly directly on group Anchor Charts.

Next, each student needs to create their own accurate digital or paper Anchor Chart to be kept as a reference in their writing journal. This will serve as a checklist during the Rough Draft stages of writing.

Once the logistics of V.O.I.C.E. can be recounted, a student can expand, condense and refine their writing for more specific purposes and complexity. Assure students that lifelong writing is a reality and they will have success if they apply what they're taught.

Now it's time to begin filling in the definitions of each element of V.O.I.C.E. and apply the skills. Supplement necessary resources to help apply the specific skill. Practice writing together and remind students that they are the author of their written work. Let students create impromtu daily questions or topics to practice the skill of the day. This builds confidence in responding to surprising Questions, Topics or Prompts thrown their way. Don't hide the practice writing. Take turns writing responses on the board then weigh the groups sample writing piece against the skill. The best examples are those created by a learning group and students are notorious for amping up the learning environment when they are a part of it.
Students learn to respond genuinely with V.O.I.C.E. and become self-reliant writers.

V.O.I.C.E. Notes
Know Your Audience and Tweak Accordingly

Voice
➡ The vibe or sound that resonates throughout the written work

Organization
➡ The sequence or arrangement of written work

Ideas
➡ Any facts and thoughts about the QTP

Conventions
➡ Spelling, Grammar, and Punctuation

Expressions
➡ Choice of words and vocabulary

Synthesize/put together the elements of V.O.I.C.E. and your message will leap from the paper straight to the mind or heart of your reader!

Voice

The author portrays, creates or uses

➡ Dialect
➡ A Vibe
➡ A Sound
➡ An Attitude

Authority, personality, and individuality are just a few effects that will travel through your written work when you write using your own Voice or one you admire.

Dialect: distinguishable language specific to a region or social group

For example, the author and poet Langston Hughes brought a unique sound and vibe to his written works. The dialect he heard as a young child was so rich he wanted to bring it out of his neighborhood and into his stories. Langston Hughes was able to relay strong messages that moved people.

Here is an excerpt from "Mother To Son" by Langston Hughes:

"Life for me ain't been no crystal stair"

This metaphor alludes to troubles that you weren't expecting and a journey ahead to overcome.

Practice Voice:

Think of a character that you know well.

Think of the meaing behind the Langston Hughes metaphor.

Keep the same message, but say or write it using the character you know well.

For example, how might an older sibling or granparent convey the same message? What sound, feeling or energy would your character use to get the same point across? Do they speak quickly, scream, have an accent, spit-talk, only recite facts?

Try to communicate the same message using the unique Voices of the characters below? Some examples have been written. Write and share your own examples restating Langston Hughes message:

Zombie Voice:
Brains don't fill you up when they are empty, yet starvation is not an option.

Fighter Pilot:
The flight has to pierce dark clouds for us to appreciate the landing.

A Scientist:
Beakers hold the contents, and we are the one's who measure.

A Librarian:

When the books are on the shelf, the words can't be seen, but their message can always be heard. Don't let the message collect dust.

An Athlete:

Sometimes sweat gets in your eyes, so you can run the distance even if you can't see the finish line.

Organization

The author
→ Structures
→ Sets-Up
→ Arranges
→ Orders
the written work.

Organization of written material varies on the written work. Have a plan based on your audience and purpose for writing. Create a Logical Sequence of events that your reader can easily follow and understand.

One tip is to allow ideas or facts that are immediately connected or dependent on one another to be written as closely together as possible.

Transition Words will help move one idea or fact on to the next keeping the written work organized and with sequence.

Examples of ways to provide structure to a written piece:

- COMPARE and CONTRAST ideas and facts
- Give a DESCRIPTION of a person, place or thing
- PERSUADE or convince an audience
- Provide CAUSE and EFFECT of an issue

Make a large 4 Square as whole group on board or in journals. Title each square using the types of structure provided. Work on the skill rather than a story. Structure responses purposefully. Sharing helps solidify learning.

Practice Organization:

COMPARE and CONTRAST

- Siblings
- Pets
- Cars
- Sports

DESCRIPTION

- A Smile
- A Frown
- A Perfect Day
- A Flavor

PERSUADE

- Your guardians to buy you a new phone
- Your teacher to allow an earned movie day
- A young child to learn how-to read
- A lawmaker to shorten or extend the school day

CAUSE and EFFECT

- Studying
- Smoking
- Texting While Driving
- Smiling Often

Ideas

The author will
- ➡ **BRAINSTORM**
- ➡ Focus on the message
- ➡ Relate to your audience

Your Ideas are the meat and potatoes of the written work. Even seasoned writers find enlightment in a Brainstorm. Always begin a written work with a Brainstorm focusing on the Question, Topic, Prompt or QTP.
Know what you want your reader to take away from your writing.
It is wonderful to think outside the box as long as you stay focused on the overall message.

Examples of what to jot down for a successful BRAINSTORM:
(No lengthy sentences in brainstorm! Think grocery list.)

- Thoughts
- Facts
- Ideas from your Schema
- Sensory words that pop into your head at thought of QTP
- Fragment of a Quote
- People or pets

Ideas are like money in the bank. Put as much in, save and use at your disposal. You will not have to use all the ideas from your BRAINSTORM, yet it is comforting to have them ready to work for you. Time the Brainstorm. Make it a game. Set the timer for a minute and see how many Ideas you can jot down. You will grow as a thinker over time and it will show in your writing!

Practice Ideas

Use a large graphic organizer to collect your Ideas. Remember, you are Storming your Brain for any and all facts, thoughts, etc., so the more the better. However, you are not competing with anyone. You are challenging yourself. Be proud of the amount of Ideas the QTP brings to your mind! Each time, try to one up your number.

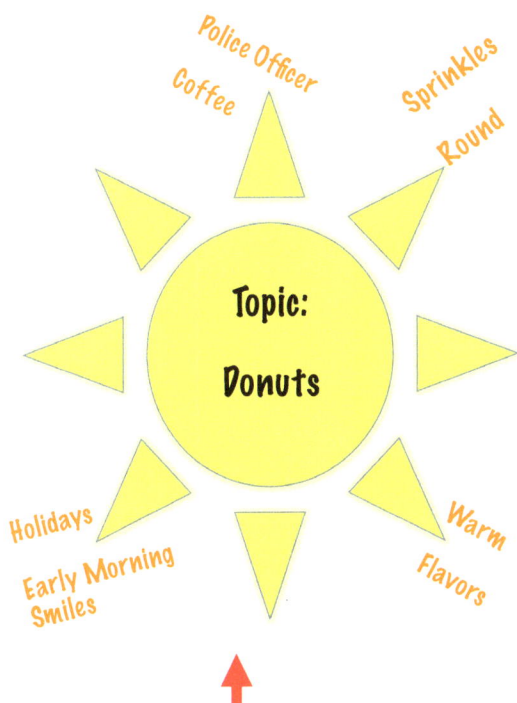

Police Officer
Coffee
Sprinkles
Round

Topic:

Donuts

Holidays
Early Morning
Smiles
Warm
Flavors

Prompt:
The importance of Pets

~ loyal

~ friendly

~ protection

~ love

~ reptiles, snakes

~ seeing eye dogs

Brainstorm Example 1:

- build confidence
- begin with a familiar topic
- this shows the benefits of using time wisely
- Timed Brainstorms allow for new ideas to enter the race
- Practice, practice and you will succeed

Brainstorm Example 2:

- builds on Structure Schema
- revisit previously discussed subjects
- In this case, we used our "Pets" Compare and Contrast
- Notice this element of V.O.I.C.E. requires it's own unique attention

Conventions

The author will use correct
- ➡ Capitalization
- ➡ Punctuation
- ➡ Verb tense

Conventions can wait until the author's last draft when checking and cleaning up a written piece is necessary. Take time to get your ideas on the paper. Conventions do effect the elements of V.O.I.C.E., so these skills should be incorporated into weekly lessons.

Grammar is critical for the Conventions skill:

- Include a good mix of complete sentences
- This can occur naturally when you begin the Rough Draft stage
- Practice writing Simple, Compound, and Complex Sentences

Streamline Point of View is also necessary:

- Verify that throughout your written work, the P.O.V. matches

Practice recognizing proper Conventions using some of the many detailed Grammar Books available or credible online resources. Keep a Reference Cheat Sheet in your Writing Journal that must be checked before you publish. Check the Dictionary for Convention Rules.

Practice Conventions

CAPITALIZATION

1) Any and all specific names and titles

2) The 1st word in any sentence

3) The pronoun "I"

PUNCTUATION

, comma

: colon

; semi-colon

" " quotation marks

. period

! exclamation point

? question mark

ALIGNED VERB TENSE

O Past
O Present
O Future

POINT OF VIEW

Identify and write
O 1st Person
O 2nd person
O 3rd person Limited
and
O 3rd person Omniscient P.O.V.'s

Expression

Incorporate:

➡ specific and precise words
➡ a message or controlling idea
➡ synonyms to emphasize and create Tone
➡ vivid word choice expanding on Ideas
➡ dialogue which adds significance
➡ supporting details
➡ rich vocabulary
➡ set the B.A.R.

Expression or Word Choice is the juiciest part of V.O.I.C.E. and can truly impact your reader. Use the dictionary and thesaurus to choose words and synonyms that enhance your purpose. Try to:

- Create an Image
- Relay an Emotion
- Deliver Facts
- Incorporate a meaningful Quote
- Eliminate Repetitive words
- Eliminate empty words by Taking Out, Replacing or Rephrasing
- set the B.A.R. : Brainstorm, Answer to why, and Research

Students who may struggle with vocabulary:

- Expand and develop Expression for ONE familiar QTP
- Describe the Image you see in your head when you hear the QTP
- Any words or phrases you can think of are important
- List any and all adjectives related to the 5 Senses focusing on QTP
- Use the Dictionary to define words central to the image you see
- Why does the QTP bring that image to mind? Write your answer.
- Is the image you see important or not? Write your answer & explain.
- Use the Dictionary again, Define words central to your explanation
- Write a few synonyms for each of your descriptve words and verbs
- Piecing these parts together will lead to a message or controlling idea

Practice Expression

Turn the Prompt "The Importance of Pets" into a question:

"Is there value or importance in having a pet?"

The goal is for classroom writers to CONNECT their Ideas with an issue, cause, relevance, or need bigger than their world. Pets provide Companionship and/or Protection which are relatable messages. V.O.I.C.E. Steps help navigate to these universal themes. Remember to set the B.A.R.. This formula has proven itself tried and true:

Brainstorm, Answers to the WHY and Research (whether definitions and synonyms or Facts) = Expression :

A student who chooses to write about a pet dog may begin:

- 4 legs, brown fur, black nose, shiny eyes, paws, fun and play
- dog watches T.V. with them
- dog waits for them to return home
- dog tail moves back and forth = happy
- dog licks = kisses
- "The importance of a pet is" ⬅ QTP ANCHOR

Always build on a Brainstorm . Ask students if the actions of a pet are important and why? One universal response is that a pet is like family or a friend. Bingo.

☐ Help the student build Expression around their ANSWER to the why
☐ Research using a Dictionary; define in writing "friend" & "family"
☐ Research the Thesaurus; write Synonyms for "friend" & "family"
☐ Research pet dogs that have made a difference (service dogs,etc.)

Begin setting the B.A.R.:

"Four legs and brown fur wait for me to return home. Whether watching T.V. or playing, those shiny eyes make me happy. My best friend is my dog."

Modeling Brainstorm & Flow of Thought
Good Practice

While our goal is self-reliant student writers, success will not happen without the Expert Learner in the classroom - the teacher. The teachers active participation in the modeling of V.O.I.C.E. is critical to the overall success of self-reliant writing.

Like any construction, the infrastructure must be made of solid components that is V.O.I.C.E.. The Expert Learner helps lay the foundation, so the student is free to design.

Again, don't hide the writing - not even yours. Step outside of comfort zones appropriately and keep moving forward even when errors and revisions in motion occur. This is Flow of Thought.

The author should:

- set the B.A.R.
- add as many details as possible
- be free to explore and embrace peer or new ideas

The author should Not be concerned with :

x Length requirements of the work
x Repetition
x Errors
x Views of others concerning the authors thought process

All efforts should maximize genuine Flow of Thought focused on setting the B.A.R.. The Flow of Thought is essentially an author's first draft and can be taught in chunks by the Expert Learner.

Errors and Revisions In Motion
Good Practice

Errors and Revisions In Motion occur during The Flow of Thought (authors first draft or Rough Draft). Errors and Revisions in Motion are good practice rather than an element necessary in a written work. Some students are a natural at these good practices. However, V.O.I.C.E. and a student's Flow of Thought can easily be hindered unless good practices are incorporated into writing instruction:

⇒ Put aside emphasis of Organization and Conventions (for now)
⇒ Set the B.A.R.
⇒ **Coherence and neatness do not fall by the wayside**
⇒ DO NOT USE YOUR ERASER OR BACK SPACE BUTTON
⇒ Keep moving foward when you make a mistake
⇒ Scratch out noticeable mistakes with 1 simple line
⇒ Move into your paper
⇒ Focus on the finish rather than the errors

Revise in motion saves time and will not interrupt Flow of Thought:

"Four legs and brown ~~hair~~ fur wait for me ~~at~~ to return home.

~~I watch and I play catch~~ Whether watching T.V. or playing, those

~~happy peppy~~ bright and shiny eyes make me happy. My ~~dog is~~

~~family~~ best friend is my dog."

Rough Draft In Layers
Good Practice

The Flow of Thought is the 1st draft or Rough Draft as previously stated. However, adding the following layers on the original draft is where progress will show. Continue to build on good practices by Layering the Rough Draft.

The writer needs to be mindful of:

➡ Due dates for Final Written Work
➡ No Rule on number of drafts neccessary
➡ Rules do apply to layering
➡ With purpose, add individual elements of V.O.I.C.E.
➡ 1st draft will be used for multiple purposes, multiple times
➡ Never copy over a 1st draft without Layering
➡ Peer/parent and teacher Revisions should be part of Layering
➡ Layering continues until controlling idea established
➡ Begin next set of Layering on 2nd Draft
➡ This process is necessary until ready to publish
➡ Use time wisely
➡ Layering can be seen and will show significant substance

Practice Rough Draft In Layers

"Four legs and brown ~~hair~~ fur wait for me ~~at~~ to return home.

~~I watch and I play catch.~~ Whether watching T.V. or playing, those

~~happy peppy~~ bright and shiny eyes make me happy. My ~~dog is~~

~~family~~ best friend is my dog."

Great start! Add 2 pieces of supporting detail for "home" & "T.V."

Student layers

Teacher layer

1) Home

it is a nice ~~feeling~~ to have someone waiting for you and ready to share your day
i have to get my siblings from bus stop, so its a ~~good feeling~~ to know my dog will be with me
who wouldn't enjoy a ~~friend~~ companion (or a kiss) waiting for them even if it does smell like dog breath

2) T.V.
so my dog can't talk to me about my favorite T.V. show, but he makes a great ~~hairy~~ furry pillow who seems to ~~like~~ bark when I laugh out loud so he does communicate

What could be one bigger message about friends? Add.

Teacher layer

Where is your re-worded Anchor?   **Peer layer**

Connect The Dots
The Way Only You Can

Students often underestimate all the wonderful experiences and knowledge contained in their Schema. And guess what? Teachers often underestimate their wonderful experiences and knowledge, as well. We are all learners and students need to know this. You can examine hundreds of sample writings and find elements of V.O.I.C.E., but hundreds more are waiting to be written. Teachers have the power to strenthen writers using the V.O.I.C.E Steps, encourage authenticity, develop complexity and contribute to a more self-reliant writer. Do not be scared of your own errors and revisions in motion. Keep scaffolding and setting the B.A.R.!
One way I make V.O.I.C.E relevant is with a large Connect the Dots visible to students. I may change the Connect the Dots from time to time, but not the message:
"We, like our writing, are a Connect the Dots. We have starting points and sometimes take a break when we come to the more confusing part of our Connect the Dots, yet a picture is still waiting to be created. We may not know the entirety of our own beautiful image just yet, but it exist and our writing is one step toward the whole. Make yours vivid and give it a V.O.I.C.E!"

It is an honor to teach and a desire to be a life-long learner. I thank the beautiful and inspiring educators I've had the opportunity to collaborate with as you are nothing less than part of the whole. Students are fortunate to have you.

www.ingramcontent.com/pod-product-compliance
Lightning Source LLC
LaVergne TN
LVHW010024070426
835508LV00001B/49